Bailey & Canteen Theme

They ride across the prairie wide,
They're always side by side,
From dawn till setting sun.
You won't see one without the other,
They're closer than brothers,
Bailey and Canteen.

Chorus:
Best friends (best friends),
Bailey and Canteen,
Best friends (best friends)—
They're brown as a berry from ridin' the prairie.
All day long, they sing this song:
"We're joined by the heart, never apart, best friends."

Bridge:
You'll never see Canteen without Bailey by his side;
They started out together and partnered up for life.
Like birds of a feather, they stick together,
Bailey and Canteen.

Except as noted below, all sound tracks and vocals recorded and mixed by Aaron Minick at The Play Room Studio, Smyrna, TN. Mastered by Marty Shrabel at AHA Productions, Goodlettsville, TN. "Bailey & Canteen Theme" audio track recorded and engineered by Mike McIntyre at Wright Studio, Nashville, TN.

Eddy Bolton: Series writer and creator; co-producer of audio tracks and story narrator.
Johnny Minick: Co-producer of audio tracks; voice for introduction.
Aaron Minick: Co-producer of audio tracks; arranged sound effects and background music; audio engineer for vocals.
Mikchael Demus: Audio engineer for music tracks.
Gus Gaches: Co-producer of audio track for "Bailey & Canteen Theme."

Musicians
Harold Bradley: Lead and rhythm guitar. Billy Linneman: Upright bass. Aaron Minick: Drums, percussion, and keyboard. Johnny Minick: Accordion and piano. Bruce Watkins: Fiddle, mandolin, lead and rhythm guitar, and upright bass. Jason Webb: Piano, strings, and keyboard.

Vocalists
Voice of Bailey: Julie Bolton. "Bailey & Canteen Theme" vocals: Eddy Bolton, Aaron Minick, and Johnny Minick. "Bailey & Canteen Theme" children's background vocals: Megan Cannon, Rachel Elrod, Kylie Gaches, Briana Sparks, Megan Watson, Brooke Welch, and Jordan Welch. "He's There" and "God Painted a Rainbow" children's background vocals: Sherry Minick, Amanda Williams, Karen Williams, and Lyndsey Williams. "God Painted a Rainbow" background vocals: Eddy Bolton, Aaron Minick, and Johnny Minick.

Special thanks to Sandy Brazile and The Bailey Hat Company, Fort Worth, Texas.
Eddy Bolton is an endorsed artist for Greg Bennett Guitars.

ISBN 0-7847-1826-1

12 11 10 09 08 07 06   9 8 7 6 5 4 3 2 1

Shelter from the Storm

STORY & SONGS BY **EDDY BOLTON**

ILLUSTRATED BY **JERRY PITTENGER**

Standard PUBLISHING
Bringing The Word to Life

Cincinnati, Ohio

The sun was already high, around mid-July—
It was hot, with nary a cloud in the sky.
Hadn't seen rain for days; Canteen was short on hay,
And even the river was dry.

Bailey told his best friends, Canteen and Lucky,
"We've drunk up our water too soon.
Before we go on our way, let's kneel down and pray
And ask God to show us which trail to choose."

Now they had just barely got up from their knees
When the sky turned dark and gray.
Then Bailey yelled out, "We've got to find shelter—
There's a sandstorm a-headin' our way!"

They ran to a cave in the side of a hill,
Where God provided a safe place to hide.

But Lucky couldn't wait for the storm to pass—
He smelled something he just had to find.

Then Bailey and Canteen got a whiff too,
So they both tagged right along behind
Till they found an old prospector cookin' up some bacon,
Grinnin' with a smile a mile wide.

He said, "Howdy, pardners! You're just in time for a meal.
My name's Ol' Tom Tumbleweed—
Folks here'bouts just call me Tom. I've always got lots of grub,
So stop by anytime for a feed."

Now little did they know, while they were eatin' that bacon
In Tom Tumbleweed's humble abode,
God answered their prayers; rain washed out the air,
And he painted the sky with a rainbow.

Well, they all said their good-byes 'neath a beautiful blue sky,
But somehow each one of them knew
They'd meet up again with Ol' Tom, their new friend,
And they sure hoped it would be real soon.

And Lucky can hardly wait to see Tom again,
'Cause he really wants some more of that bacon!

Round up all these Bailey & Canteen adventures!

Canyon Rescue!
STORY & SONGS BY EDDY BOLTON   ILLUSTRATED BY JERRY PITTENGER
0-7847-1824-5

Lost and Found
STORY & SONGS BY EDDY BOLTON   ILLUSTRATED BY JERRY PITTENGER
0-7847-1825-3

Shelter from the Storm
STORY & SONGS BY EDDY BOLTON   ILLUSTRATED BY JERRY PITTENGER
0-7847-1826-1

On the Range
0-7847-1851-2

Roundup!
0-7847-1850-4

Visit your local Christian bookstore or www.standardpub.com or call 1-800-543-1353.